Mac
Our Pet Raven

Ravens are curious, just like kids! Some kids think ravens look mean and scary.
But ravens are not mean or scary at all.
Ravens are very friendly and love to be around people.
Ravens are also super smart!

$9.99 USD

Dedication

Text copyright—2015 by Linda Sund

Illustrations copyright—2015 by Denis Proulx and Linda Sund

All rights reserved. No part of this book may be reproduced by any means whatsoever, either mechanical or electronic, (except for brief portions for the purpose of review), without permission of the publisher.

For further information, write to MAC THE RAVEN ENTERPRISES, LLC

P.O. Box 1186

Hoodsport, WA

lindalsund@gmail.com

www.mactheraven.com

Library of Congress Control Number: TXu 1-863-507

International Standard Book Number: 978-0-9893597-9-5

Mac Meets Leeanne

Our Pet Raven – Based On A True Story

Written By Linda Sund

Illustrated by Denis Proulx

More stories of Mac's Adventures:

Meet Mac
Mac Learns To Fly
Mac and Clinger
Mac Meets Fern

Order online
www.mactheraven.com

Coming Soon:

Mac's First Day At School,
Mac Hikes Mt Ellinor
and more!

With much thanks to Denis Proulx for creating Mac and all of his family and friends. I believe Leeanne is extremely unique and will be well loved by all.
Especially for: Rylee, Kale, Sarah, and Trevor

Love, Nana & Papa

Mac, our pet raven,
was enjoying the sunny day
after his morning bath.
What was he going to do, Mac thought?!
I wish I had a visitor.
Suddenly, he heard a loud noise.
It's Leeanne! She has come over to play.
Leeanne has long blond hair with ringlets,
and bright blue eyes.
She is wearing a pretty blue and white dress.
Today is extra special.
Leeanne turned 5 years old today!
She got tap shoes for her birthday.

Leeanne tells Mac,
"I am going to learn how to dance!"
Mac thinks . . . I can dance! I can dance!
Let me show you how!
Mac jumps and jumps for her to see.
Here I go! Watch me rock! Watch me roll!
Look at me, I've got soul!!

There is Mac,
showing off what he knows.
Mac hops left, then he hops right.
He is dancing like his legs are stiff and tight!
Leeanne starts to turn and twirl, twirl, twirl!
Mac gets dizzy
watching her swirl.

Next she tells Mac:
"Guess what else?
I want to be a Campfire Girl!
Not a Brownie! Or a Girl Scout!

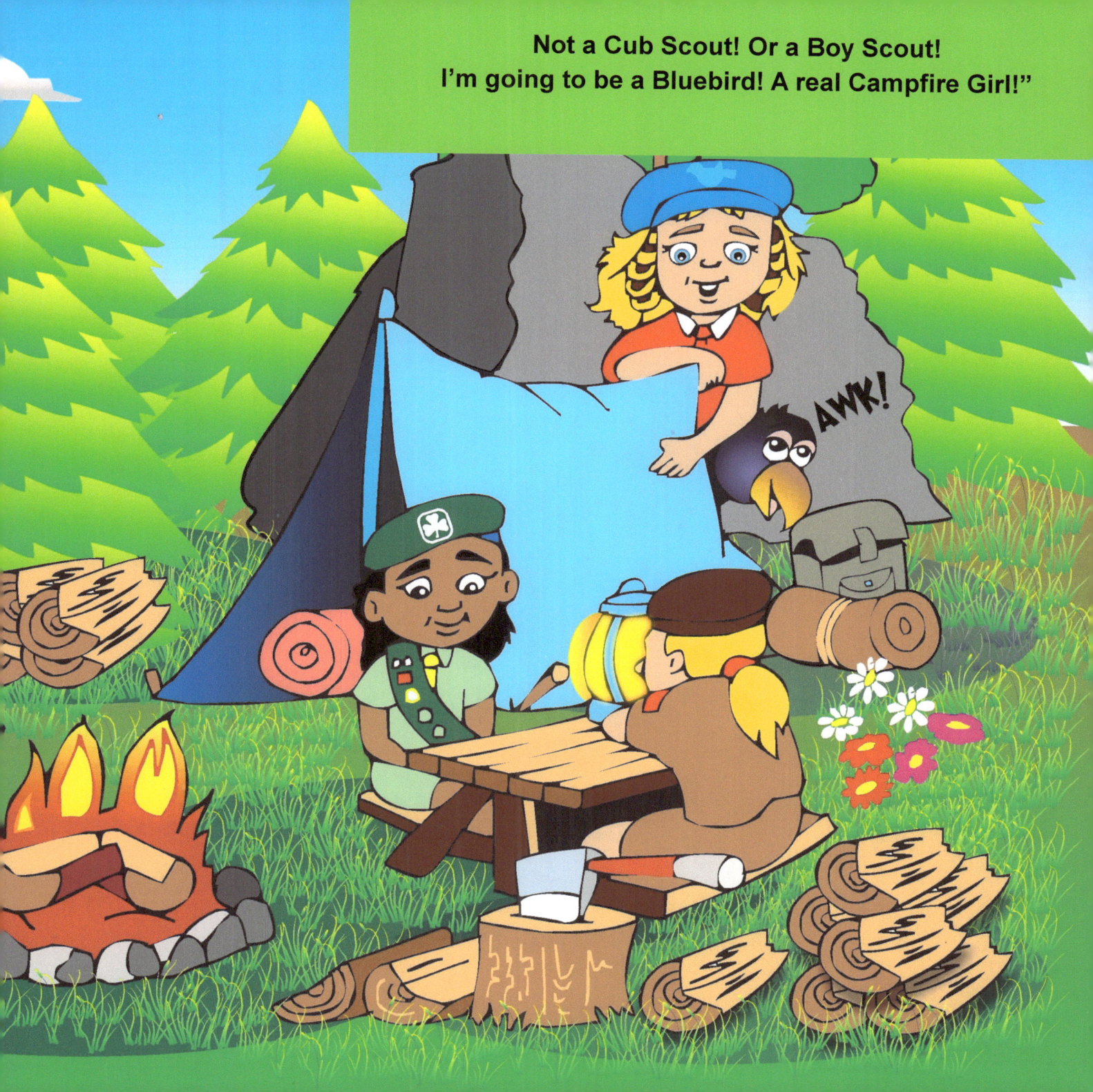

"Guess what else?" Leeanne tells Mac.
"Now that I'm five I get to go to school. I'm going to learn to read and write.
I might even learn to fly a kite!"

Mac is thinking about going to school. He wants to do that too!
Are there any rules about birds in school?

Mac thinks . . .
Maybe his friend Fern, the deer,
would like to go to school too.
Here she comes now!
Leeanne smiles and says,
"Fern, I'm happy to see you!
I'm sorry you got hurt by that speeding car.
I'm glad Papa Brian showed up when he did.
He rescued you!"
Than Leeanne reaches over
to give Fern a big, gentle hug.

Mac wants a hug too.
After all, he is shiny and clean.
Mac flaps his wings, thinking . . .
Leeanne! I'm down here,
pay attention to me!
Leeanne bends over to pick up Mac.
Mac starts to cry. "AWK! AWK! AWK!"
That really does hurt!
A little too much squeezing for this little bird.

Leeanne hugs Mac tight, like her dolly.

He doesn't think it's so funny.

He's not a doll.

Be careful! Don't squeeze his tummy.

Mac thinks to himself . . .

Leeanne needs a lesson

on how to pick up a bird.

Be gentle. Pay attention.

Don't squeeze too tight!

Leeanne starts over. Now she knows.

Mac hops on!

All the way up her arm he goes!

Mac gets to her shoulder,

and Leeanne shouts with glee,

"Look! I have a bird on me!"

Clinger, the mischievous cat,
and Ruby come over
to see what all the fuss is about.
Ruby brings her ball
so she and Leeanne can play.
Papa Brian says,
"Oh Ruby! So sorry!
It's time for Leeanne to go."
Mama Linda smiles and says,
"She will come back to play with you
some other sunny day!"

Papa Brian and Mama Linda wave goodbye!

They all watch as Leeanne's car slowly drives away.

Mac flies above the car, until he reaches the old growth tree.

Mac screeches: "AWK! AWK! AWK!" Leeanne looks up and gives Mac a friendly wink. Mac looks down wondering . . . Can she see me?

Mac sits in the tree and watches the car
until he can no longer see it.
His brand new friend
disappears down the long driveway.
Leeanne will visit again, on another day.
Maybe she will come back
on her next birthday!
Or, just maybe,
Mac will be with Leeanne
at school someday.

More of Mac's Adventures To Come!

Mac and Leeanne

www.mactheraven.com

www.ingramcontent.com/pod-product-compliance
Lightning Source LLC
Chambersburg PA
CBHW040022050426
42452CB00002B/99